A APPLE PIE

By
KATE GREENAWAY

DERRYDALE BOOKS   NEW YORK • AVENEL, NEW JERSEY

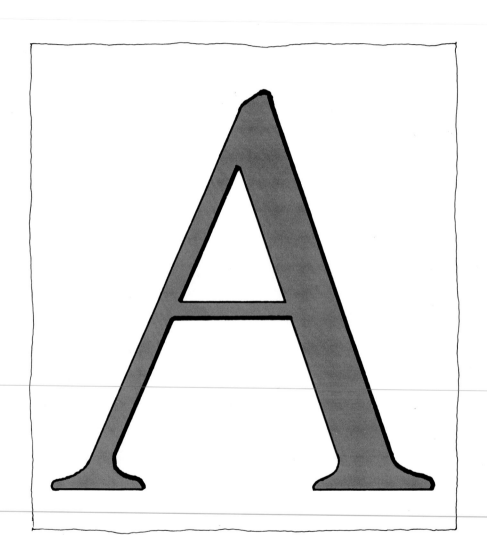

A APPLE PIE

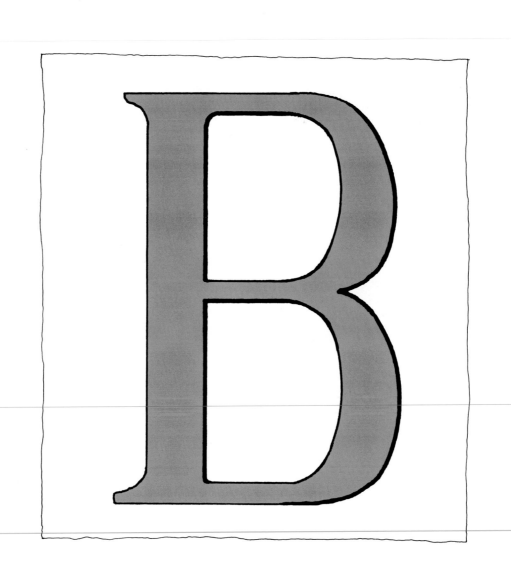

B

B BIT IT

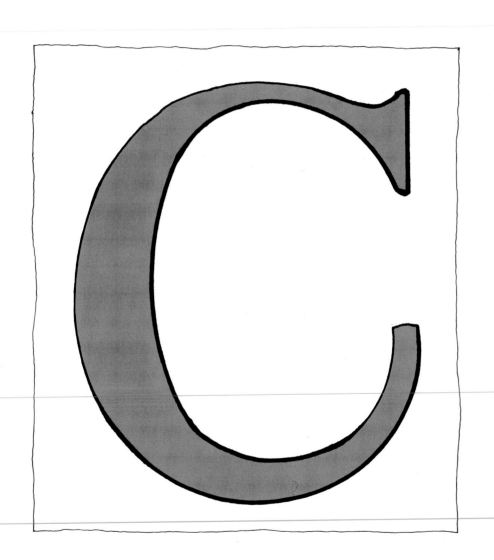

C CUT IT

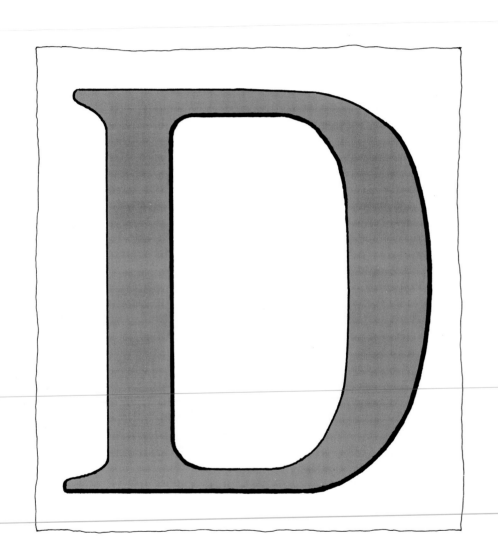

D DEALT IT

E

E

EAT IT

KG

F

FOUGHT FOR IT

G GOT IT

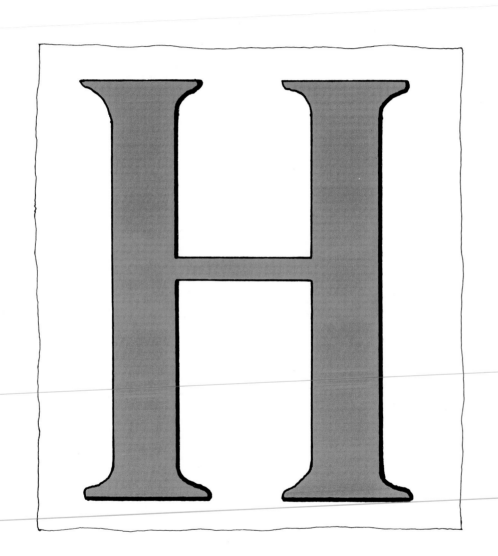

H HAD IT

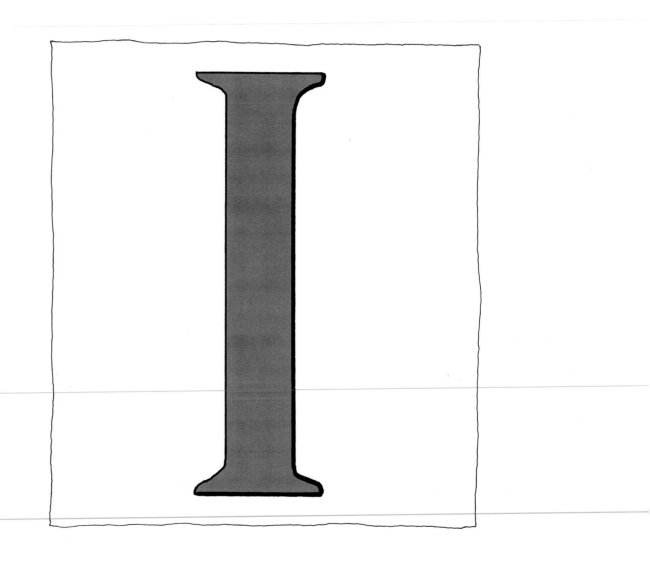

I INSPECTED IT

J JUMPED FOR IT

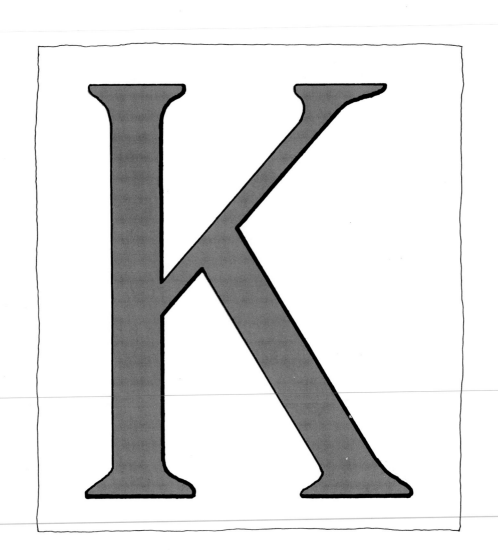

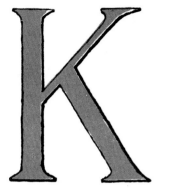 **K** KNELT FOR IT

L LONGED FOR IT

M MOURNED FOR IT

N NODDED FOR IT

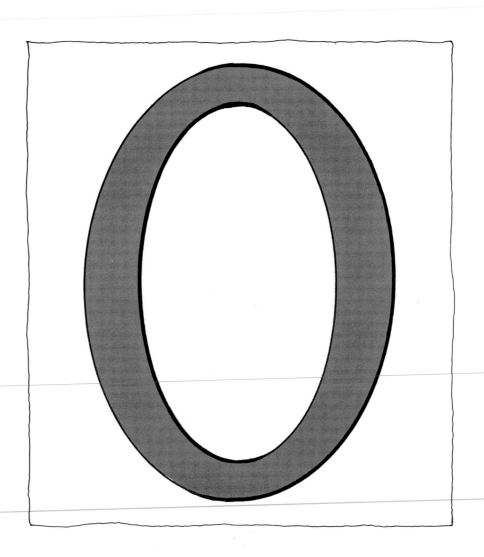

OPENED IT

P PEEPED IN IT

Q QUARTERED IT

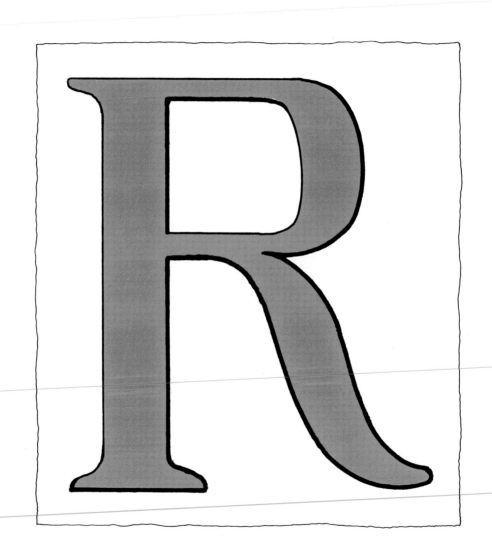

R RAN FOR IT

S SANG FOR IT

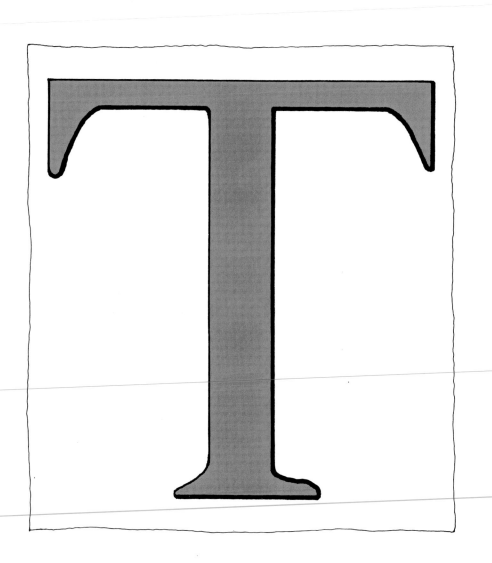

T TOOK IT

UVW
XYZ

U V W X Y Z

ALL HAD A LARGE SLICE
AND WENT OFF TO
BED